A MODERN METHOD FOR GUITAR

rock songbook volume 1

Songs by
The Beatles
Creedence Clearwater Revival
The Rolling Stones
Santana
Stone Temple Pilots
The Who
And Other Rock Greats

Based on the Best-Selling Method by
william leavitt

Berklee Press

Vice President: David Kusek
Dean of Continuing Education: Debbie Cavalier
Assistant Vice President/CFO: Robert F. Green
Managing Editor: Jonathan Feist
Editorial Assistants: Jimmy Haas, Won (Sara) Hwang, Jacqueline Sim, Andrea Penzel
Cover Designer: Kathy Kikkert
Compiled by Scotty Johnson

ISBN 978-0-87639-119-8

1140 Boylston Street
Boston, MA 02215-3693 USA
(617) 747-2146

Visit Berklee Press Online at
www.berkleepress.com

DISTRIBUTED BY

HAL•LEONARD®
CORPORATION
7777 W. BLUEMOUND RD. P.O. BOX 13819
MILWAUKEE, WISCONSIN 53213

Visit Hal Leonard Online at
www.halleonard.com

Contents

Foreword

This collection of rock songs has been compiled as a companion to Modern Method for Guitar: Volume 1. William Leavitt's series has been one of the most influential guitar methods ever published. It has been at the core of guitar instruction at Berklee College of Music for decades, translated into several languages, and used worldwide by more than half a million guitarists, many of whom have become world renowned artists. Volume 1 will give you the technique necessary to perform a lot of great music.

The importance of applying what you learn cannot be overstated, and this songbook is designed to help you do just that. Learning songs breathes life into the rudimentary exercises that are the cornerstone of building technique and confidence. It has always been the song that brings everything together, and playing songs is often when we find true inspiration.

The following collection includes classic and recent rock guitar anthems that will help you experience the reward of playing rhythm guitar and single-note riffs. These songs also make great jam tracks to help you develop your improvisational skills.

I hope you enjoy "sitting in" with all of this timeless music. I know it will help you utilize and enjoy all of the musical techniques that you are learning.

Scotty Johnson
Associate Professor, Guitar
Berklee College of Music

Are You Gonna Go My Way

Words by Lenny Kravitz
Music by Lenny Kravitz and Craig Ross

TRACK 1

to save the day.　　　And　I won't leave un - til I'm　done.

G7

So　that's　why _____　　　you　got　to　try.

*T = Thumb on 6th str.

You　got　to breathe and have some　fun.

Though I'm not paid, ____ I play this game. And I won't stop un-til I'm

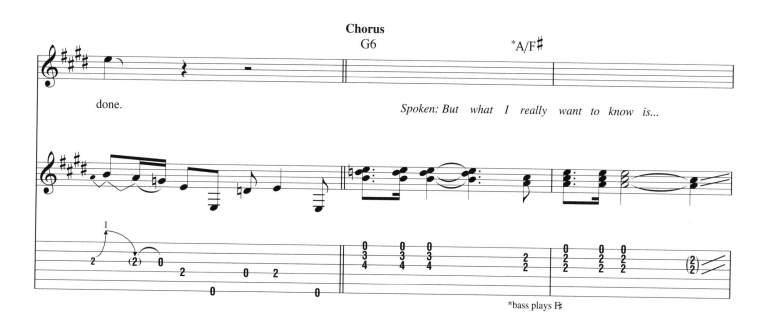

done.

Chorus
G6   *A/F♯

Spoken: But what I really want to know is...

bass plays F♯

E   D   E   G   E   *To Coda*

Are you gon-na go my way?

Interlude

And I got to, got to know, — yeah.

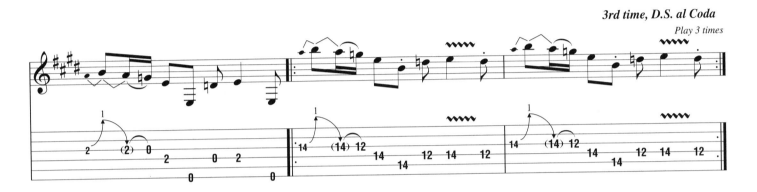

3rd time, D.S. al Coda

Play 3 times

Coda

And I got to, got to know. ___

Interlude

Guitar Solo

Play 4 times

w/ flanger

flanger off

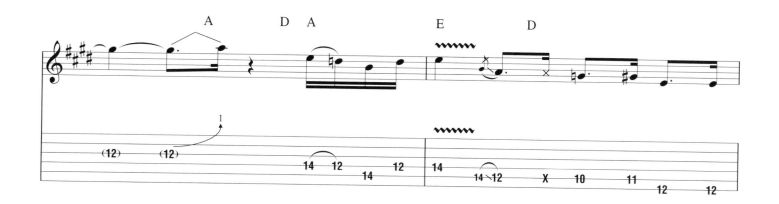

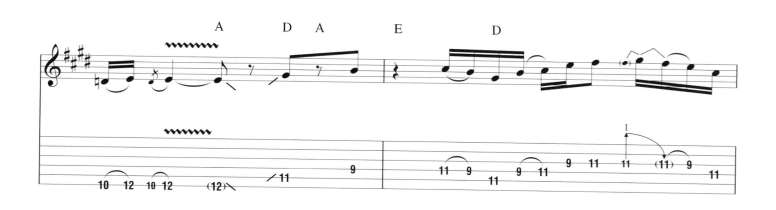

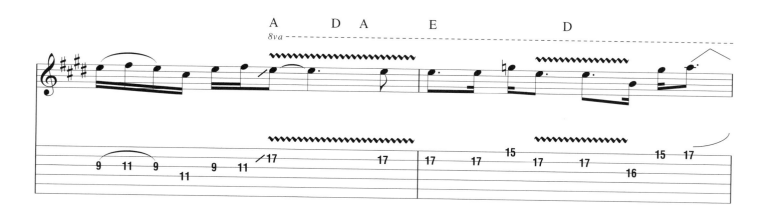

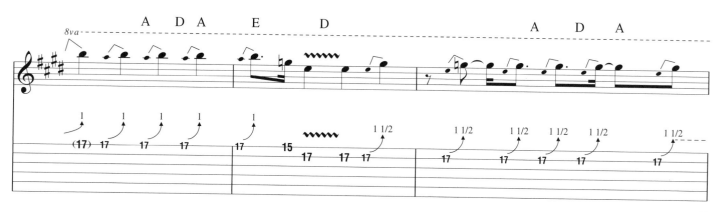

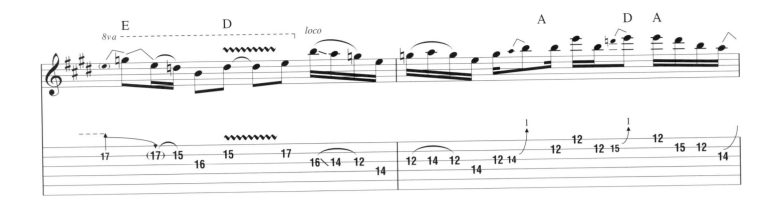

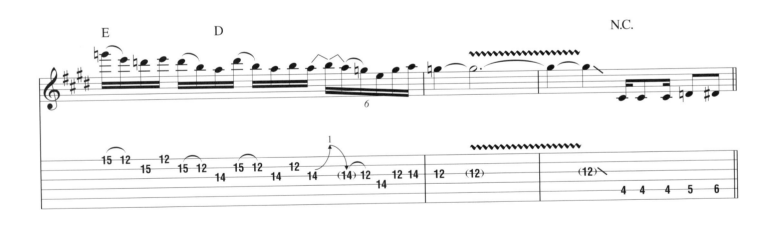

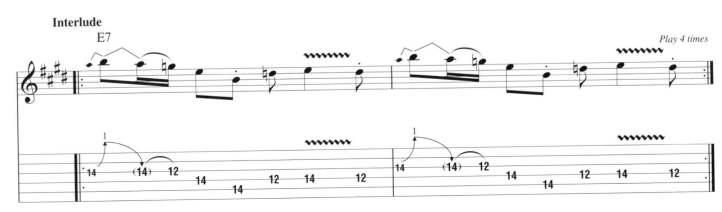

Outro-Chorus

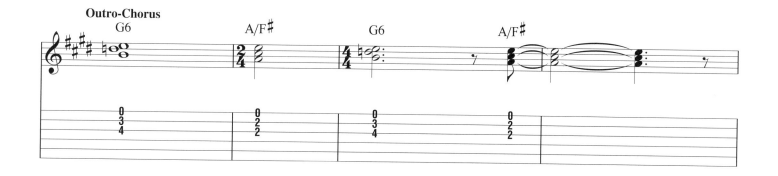

Are you gon-na go my way?

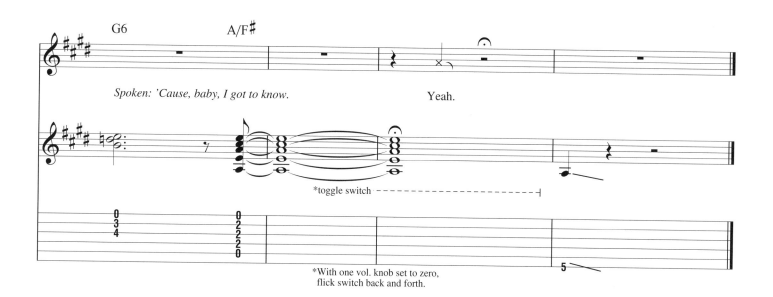

Spoken: 'Cause, baby, I got to know.

Yeah.

*toggle switch

*With one vol. knob set to zero,
flick switch back and forth.

Additional Lyrics

2. I don't know why we always cry.
   This we must leave and get undone.
   We must engage and rearrange
   And turn this planet back to one.
   So tell me why we got to die
   And kill each other one by one.
   We've got to hug and rub-a-dub.
   We've got to dance and be in love.

Beast of Burden

TRACK 2

Words and Music by Mick Jagger and Keith Richards

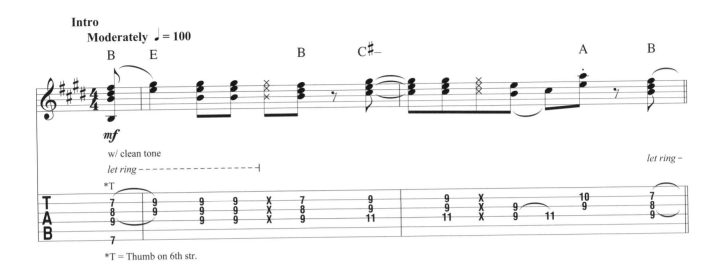

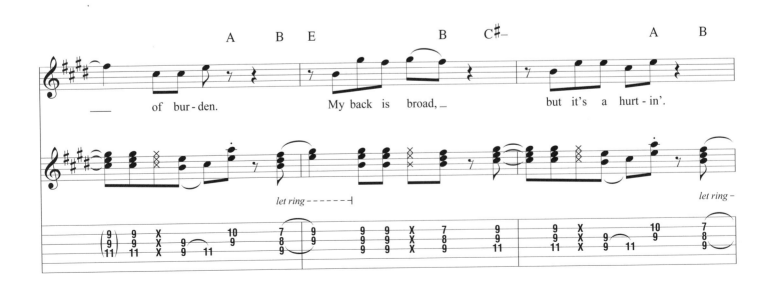

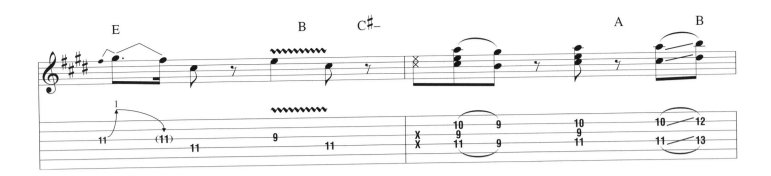

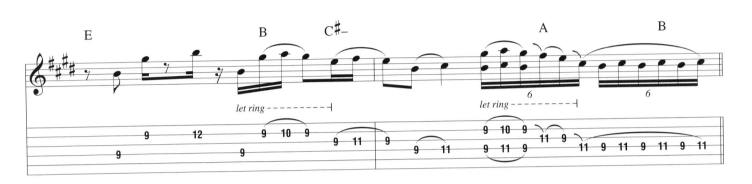

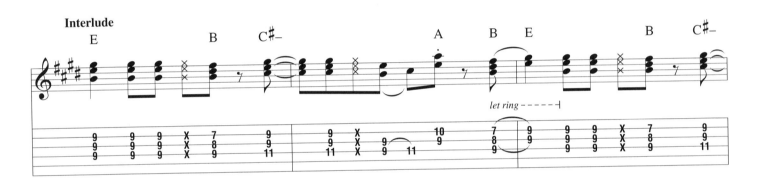

Interlude

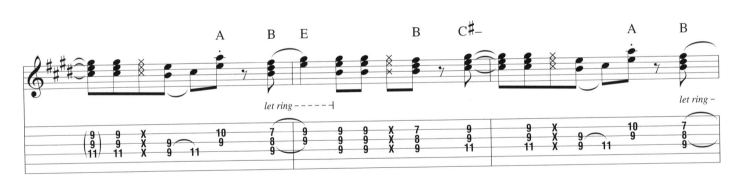

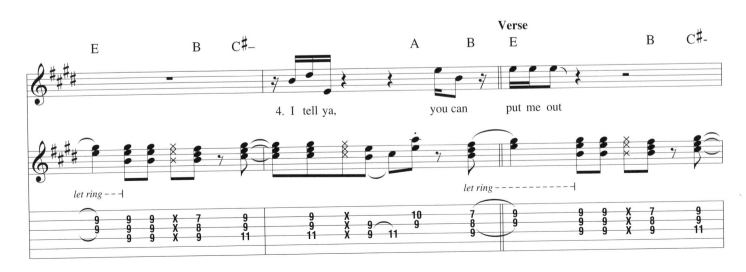

Verse

4. I tell ya,   you can   put me out

you to make love to me. ___ Uh. Yeah. ___

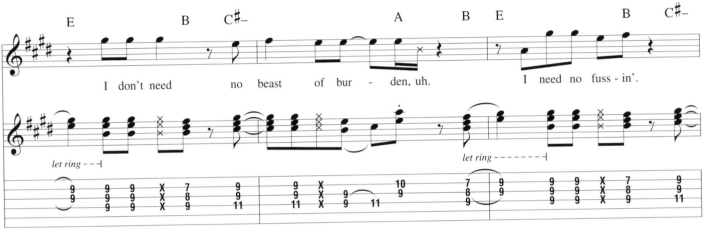

I don't need no beast of bur - den, uh. I need no fuss - in'.

I need no nurs - in'. Nev - er, nev - er, nev - er, nev - er, nev - er need. ___

Repeat and fade

La Bamba

By Ritchie Valens

Intro
Moderately fast Rock ♩ = 140

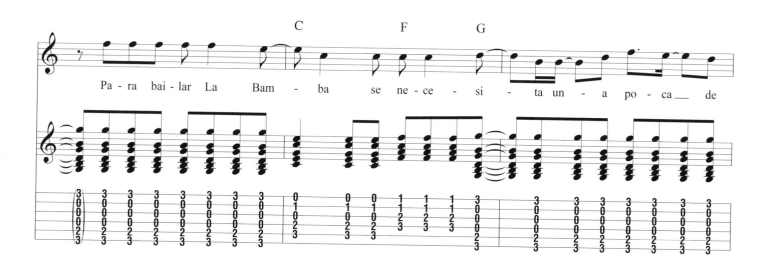

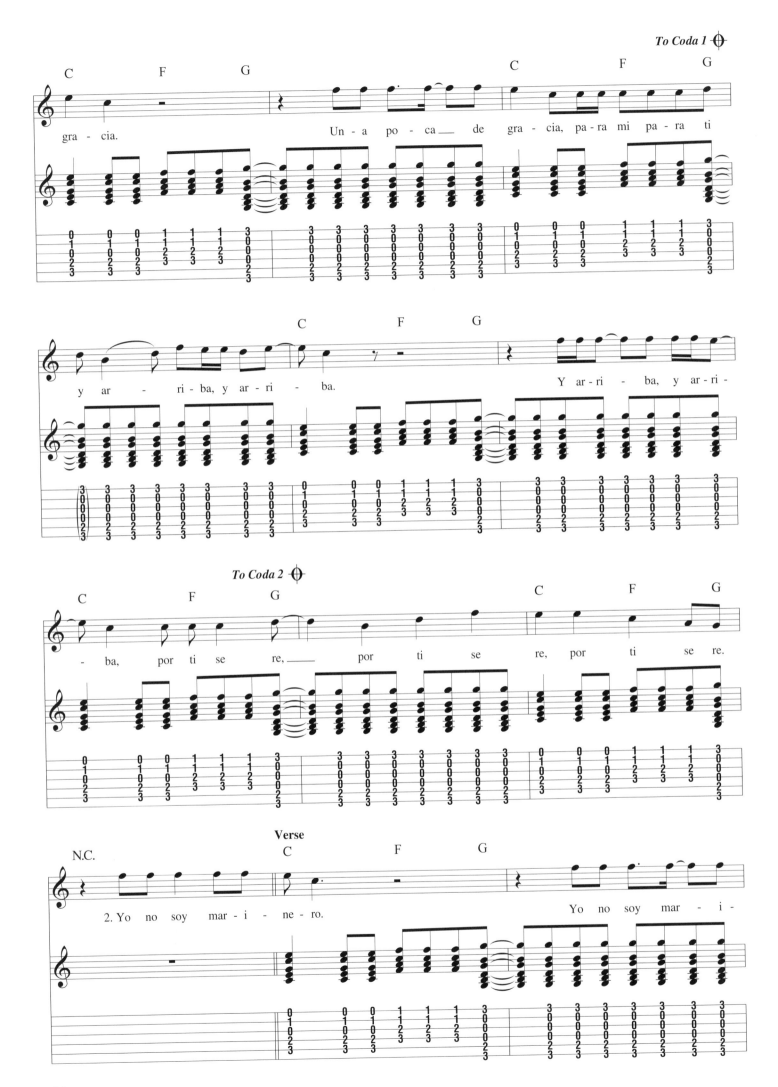

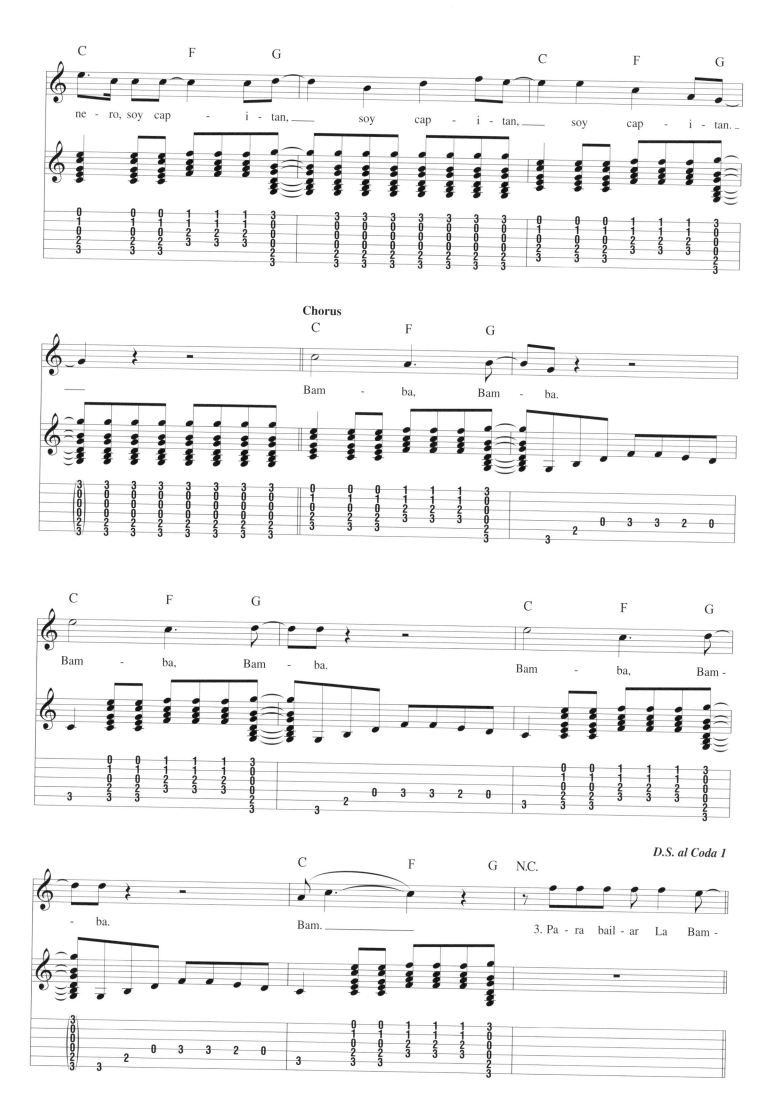

Coda 1

D.S. al Coda 2

Coda 2

4. Pa - ra bail - ar La

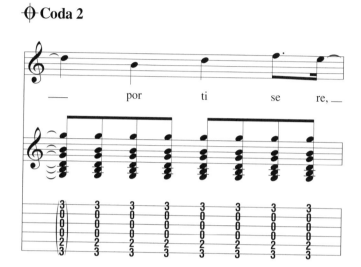

— por ti se re, —

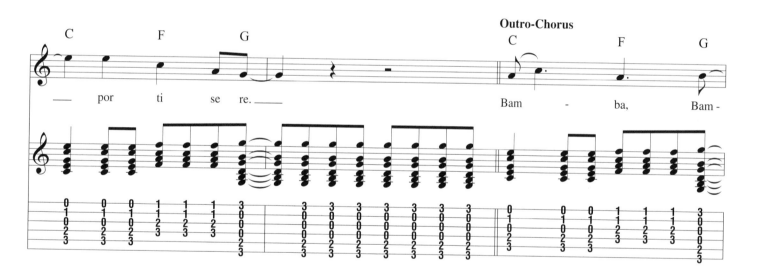

— por ti se re. — Bam - ba, Bam -

Outro-Chorus

Repeat and fade

- ba. Bam - ba, Bam - ba.

Born on the Bayou

Words and Music by John Fogerty

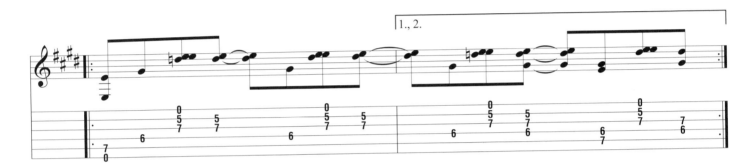

ou, Lord, Lord.

ou. Gon - na run, go. Doot,

Guitar Solo

E7

w/ slight dist.

let ring ------- *let ring -*

let ring ----

w/ fingers

let ring -- *let ring* --

Interlude

E7

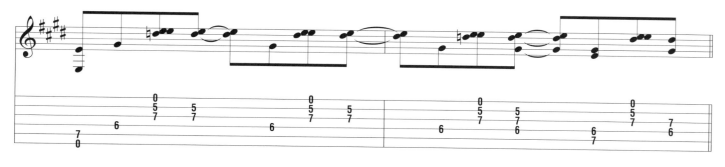

Interlude

E

Play 4 times

Spoken: Oh get back,

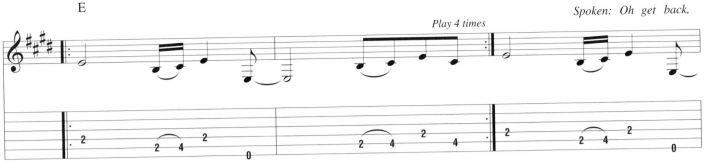

boy!

D   A   E   E7

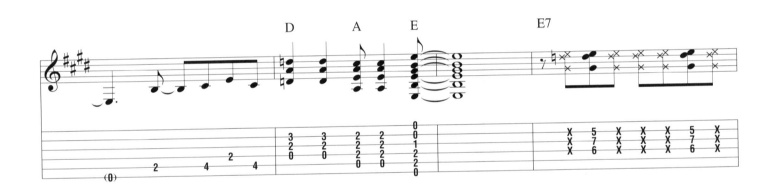

34

D.S. al Coda

4. Well,

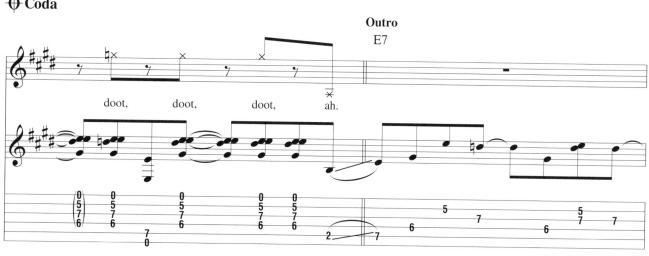

Coda

Outro
E7

doot,   doot,   doot,   ah.

Repeat and fade

TRACK 5

Brown Eyed Girl

Words and Music by Van Morrison

Intro
Moderately fast Rock ♩ = 144

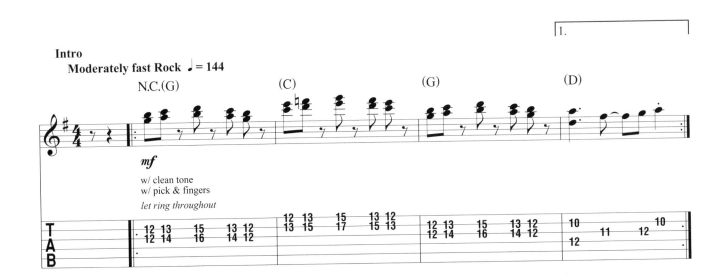

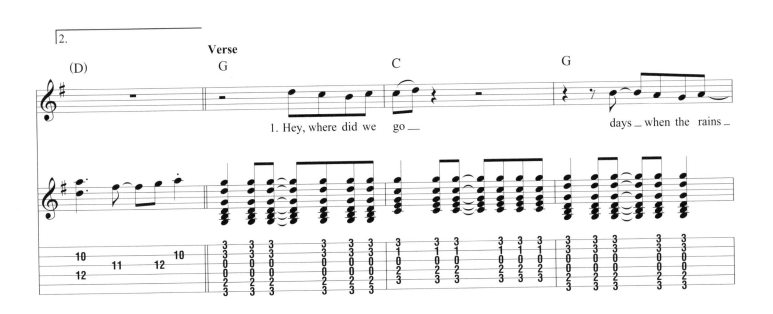

1. Hey, where did we go ___ days ___ when the rains ___

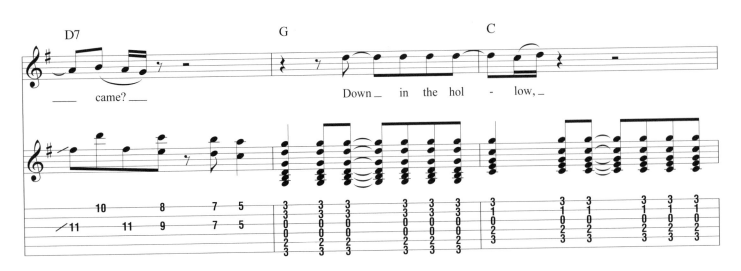

___ came? ___ Down ___ in the hol - low, ___

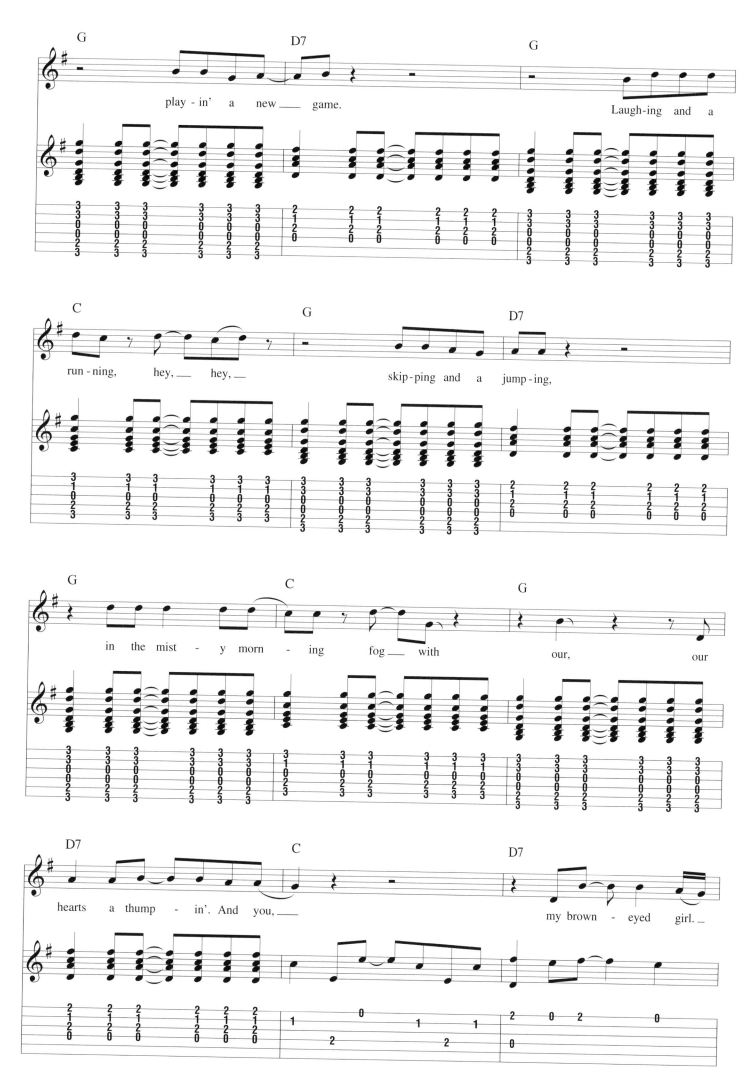

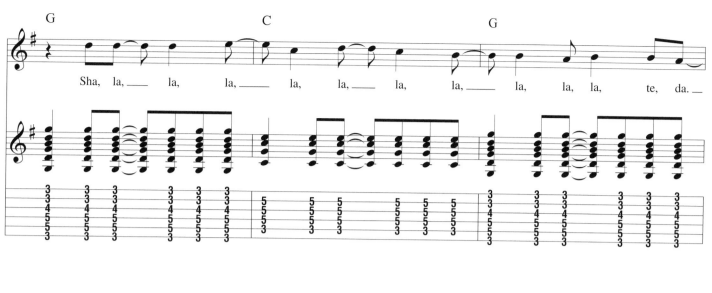

Sha, la, ___ la, la, ___ la, la, ___ la, la, ___ la, la, la, te, da. ___

___ La, te, da. ___

Bass Interlude

N.C.(G)   (C)   (G)   (D7)

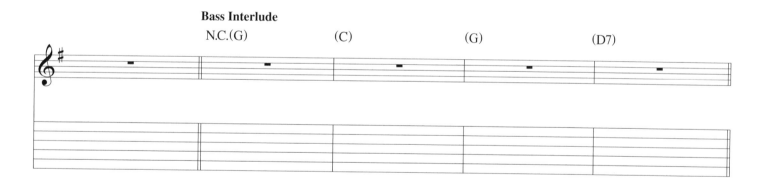

Verse

3. So hard   to find _____ my way   now ___ that I'm all ___

Day Tripper

Words and Music by John Lennon and Paul McCartney

Intro
Moderate Rock ♩ = 138

Verse

1. Got a good rea - son for tak - ing the ea - sy way out.
2.,3. (See additional lyrics)

— Got a good rea - son for

Breakdown

D.S. al Coda
(take 1st ending)

⊕ Coda

Interlude

Play 4 times

Repeat and fade

Outro

Day trip - per.   Day trip - per, yeah. __

Additional Lyrics

2. She's a big teaser.
     She took me half the way there.
     She's a big teaser.
     She took me half the way there, now.

3. Tried to please her,
     She only played one night stands.
     Tried to please her,
     She only played one night stands, now.

Interstate Love Song

Words and Music by Dean De Leo, Robert De Leo, Eric Kretz and Scott Weiland

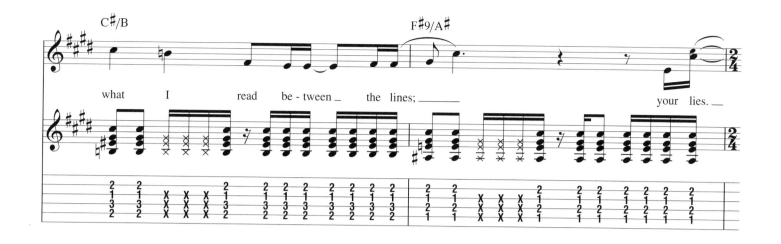

what I read be-tween _ the lines; _____ your lies. _

3rd time, To Coda 1

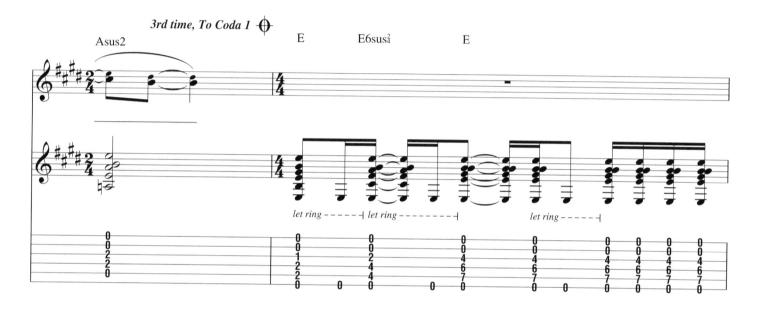

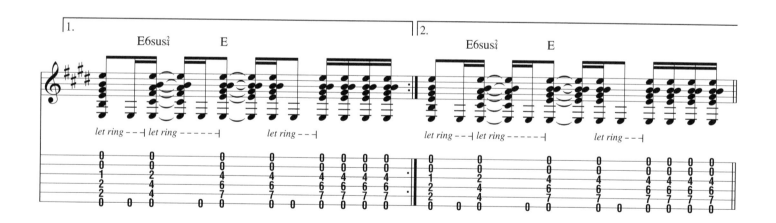

Interlude

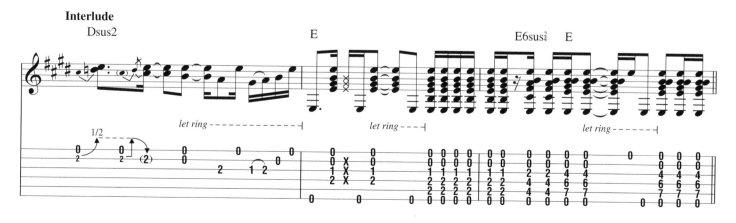

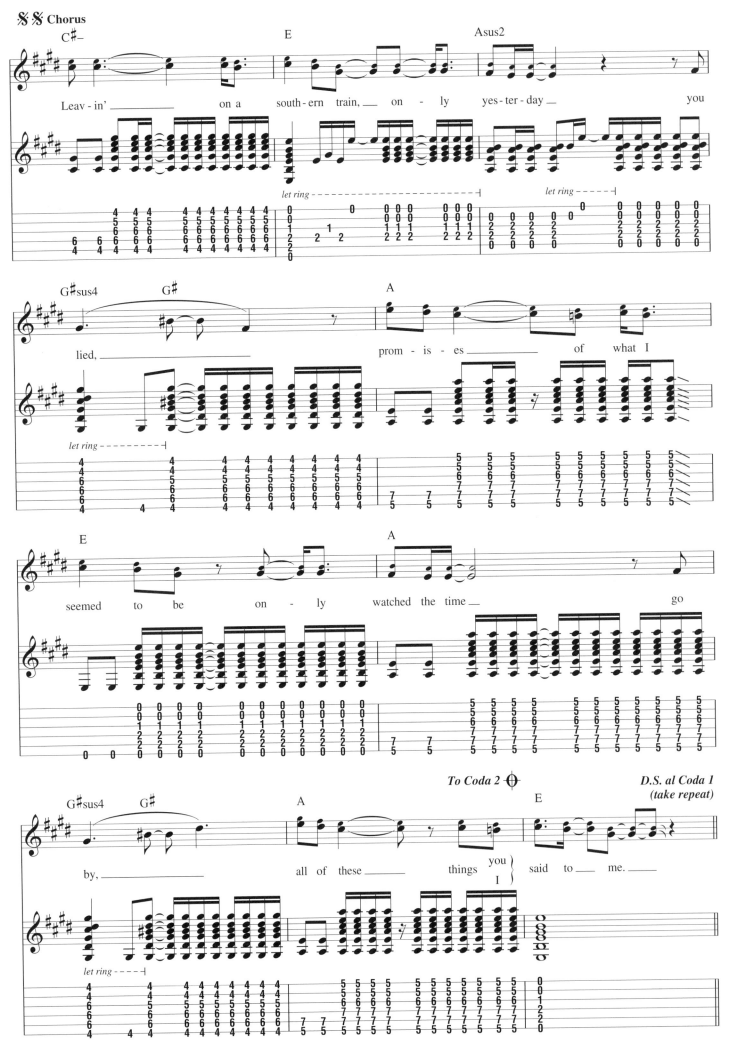

⊕ Coda 1

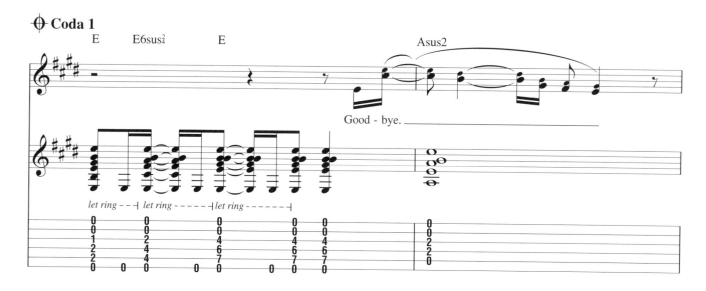

Good - bye. _____

D.S.S. al Coda 2

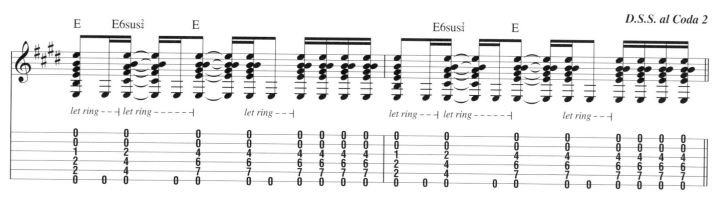

⊕ Coda 2

Outro

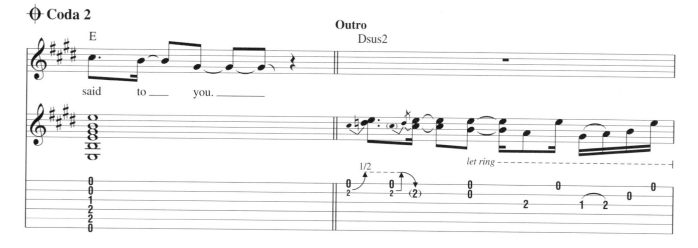

said   to ___   you.

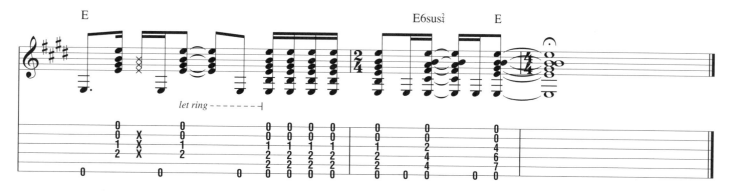

Additional Lyrics

2. Feelin', a, like a hand in rusted shame,
So do you laugh or does it cry? Reply?

3. Breathin' is the hardest thing to do,
With all I've said and all that's dead for you; you lied.

Mary Had a Little Lamb

Written by Buddy Guy

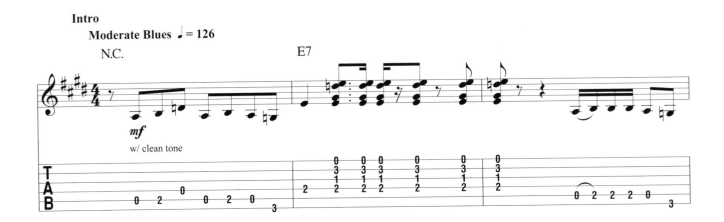

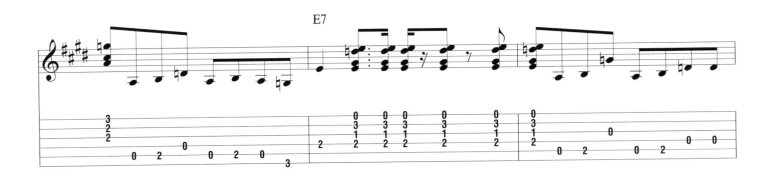

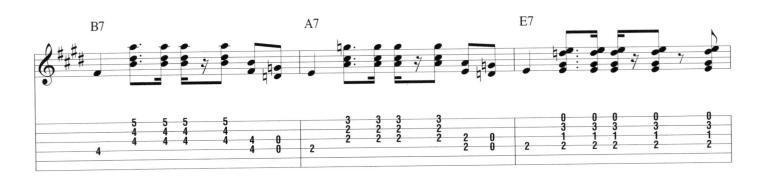

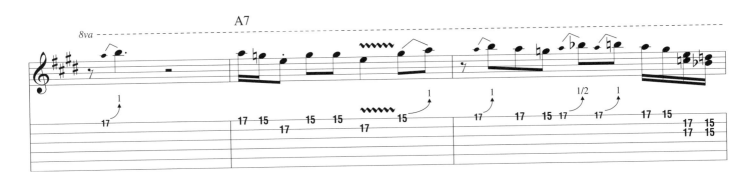

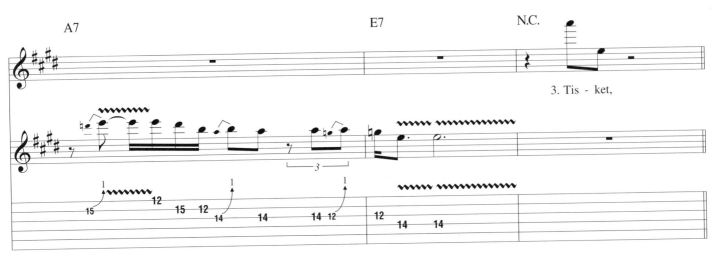

3. Tis - ket,

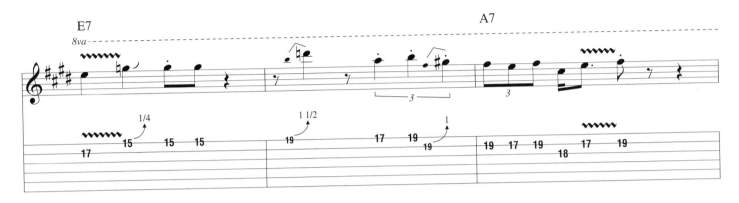

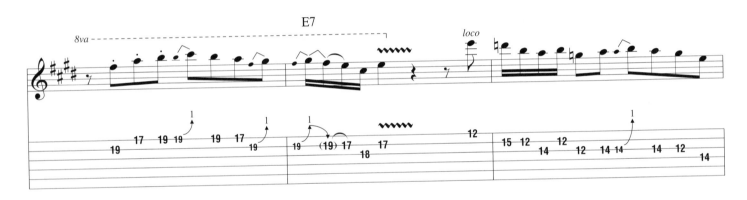

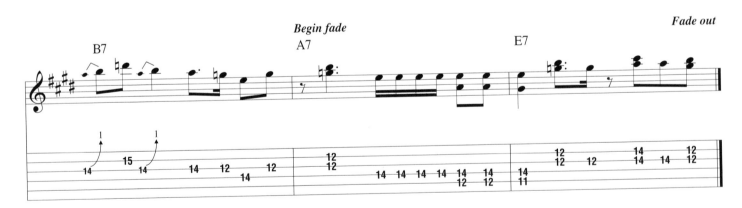

Additional Lyrics

2. He followed her to school one day
And broke the teacher's rule.
And what a time did they have
That day at school.

4. No, no, no, no, no, no, oo.
No, no, no, no, yeah.
No, no, no, no, no, yeah.
No, no, no, no, no, no, yeah.
Uh, uh, uh, uh. Hit it.

TRACK 9

Oye Como Va

Words and Music by Tito Puente

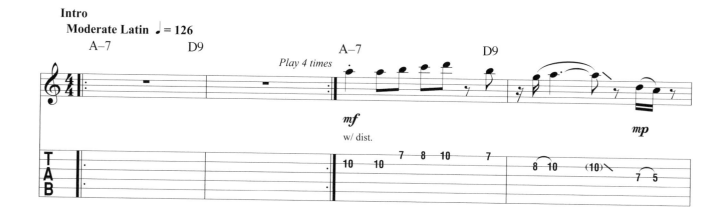

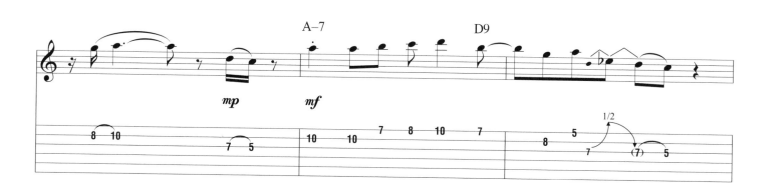

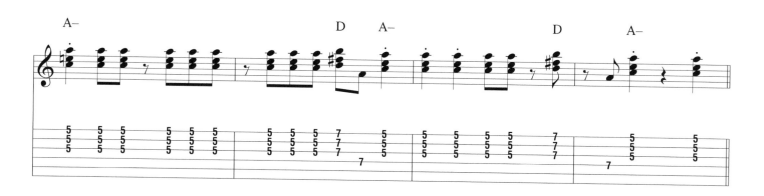

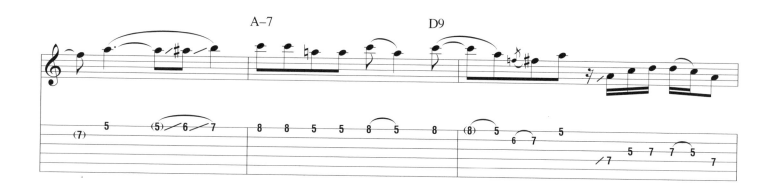

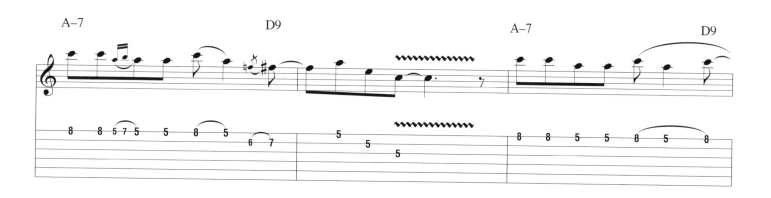

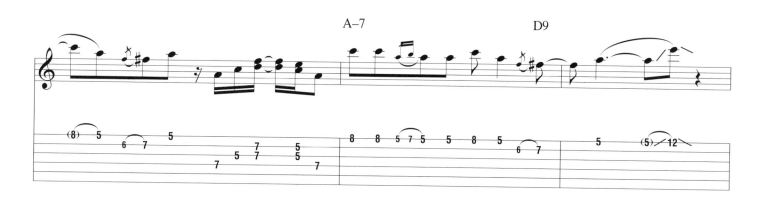

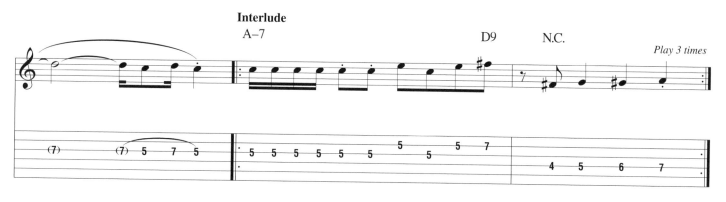

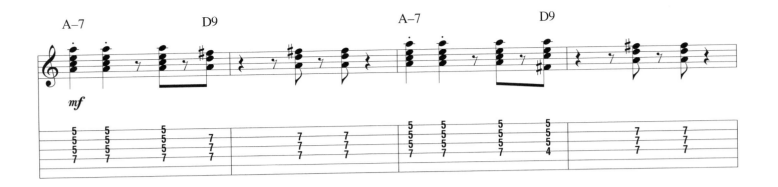

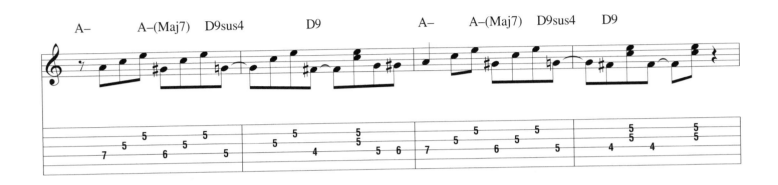

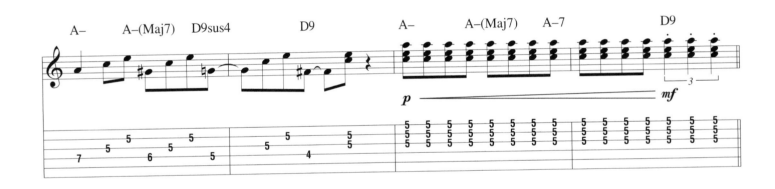

Organ Solo

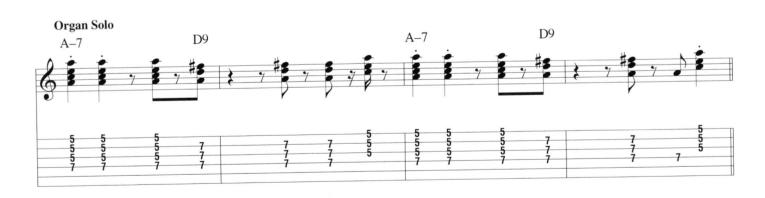

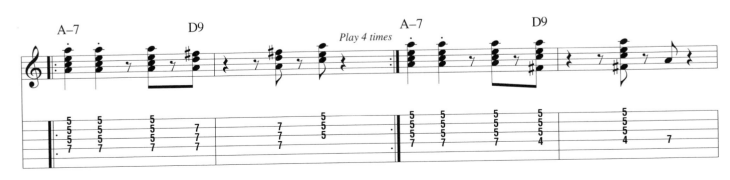

Bridge

Guitar Solo

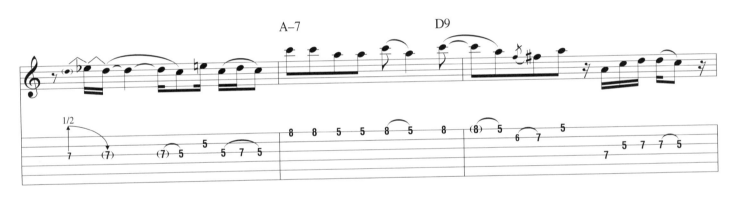

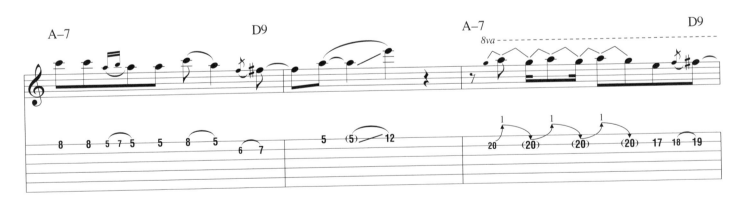

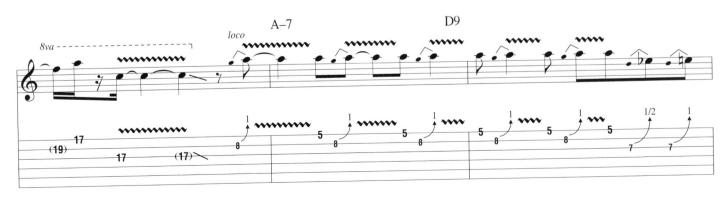

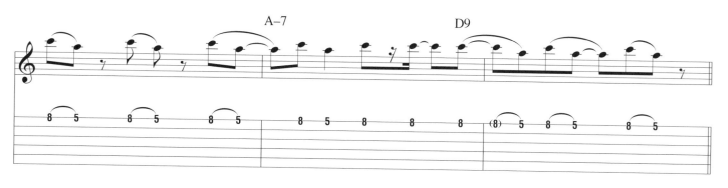

Outro

Uh!

My Girl

Words and Music by William "Smokey" Robinson and Ronald White

sun - shine _____ on a cloud - y day. _____

2. *See additional lyrics*

When it's cold out - side, _____ I've ___ got the

(My girl.)   talk - in' 'bout _____ my _____ girl. _____   (My girl.)

Outro

w/ Voc. ad lib., till fade

DMaj7

Repeat and fade

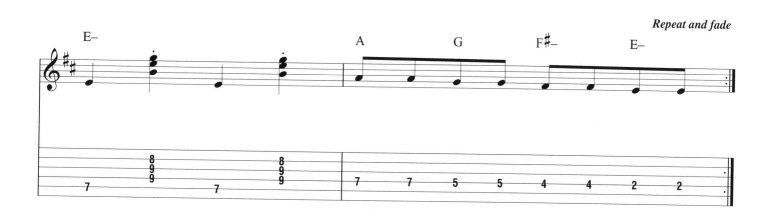

Additional Lyrics

2. I've got so much honey the bees envy me.
    I've got a sweeter song than the birds in the tree.

Pinball Wizard

Words and Music by Peter Townshend

Intro
Moderately ♩ = 132

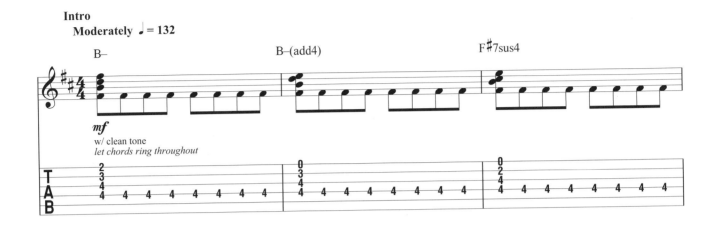

*T = Thumb on 6th string.

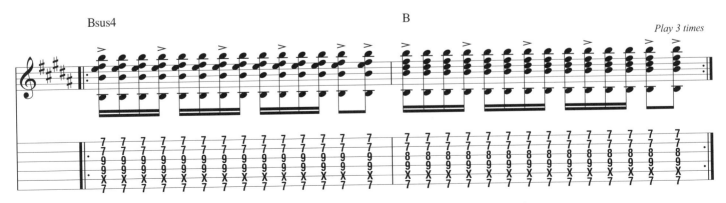

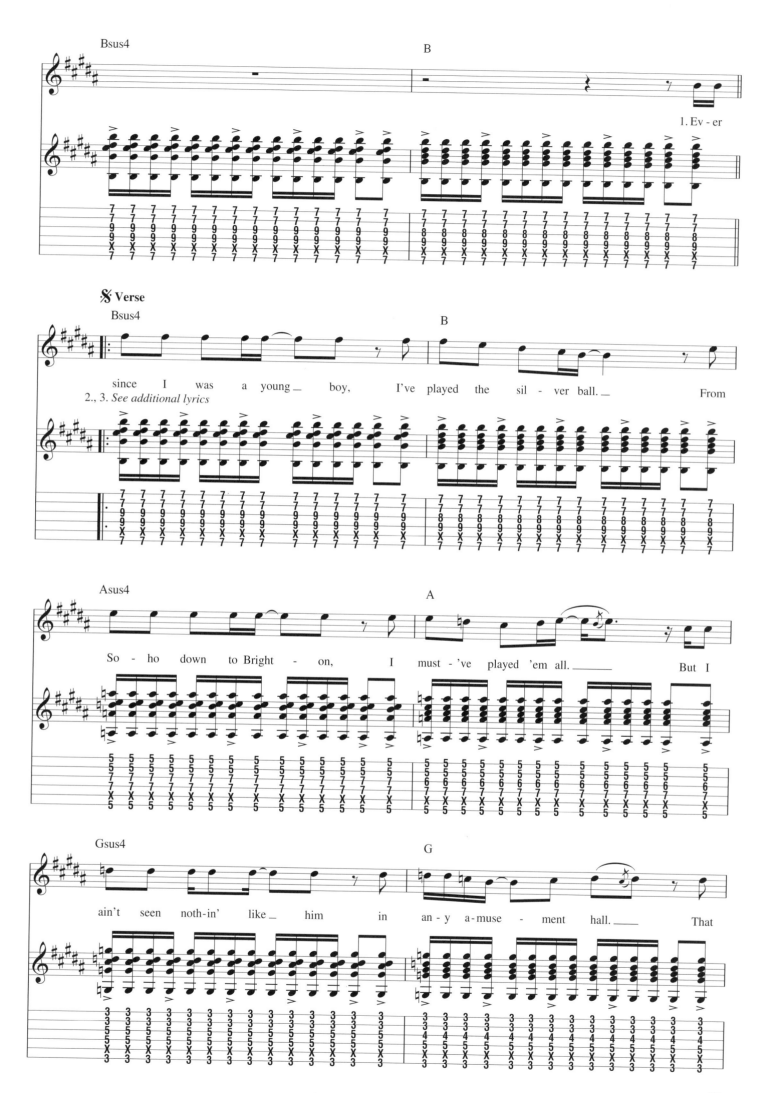

Bridge

How do you think ___ he does ___ it?
(I don't ___ know.) ___

D.S. al Coda
(take 2nd ending)

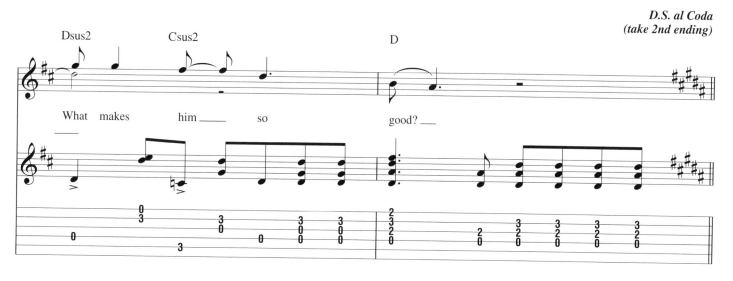

What makes him ___ so good? ___

⊕ **Coda**

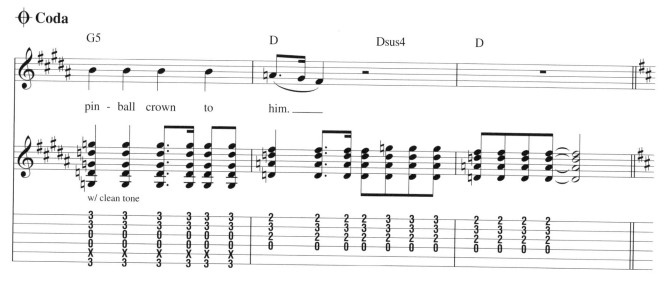

pin - ball crown to him. ___

w/ clean tone

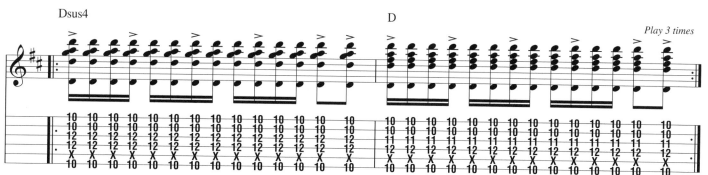

Play 3 times

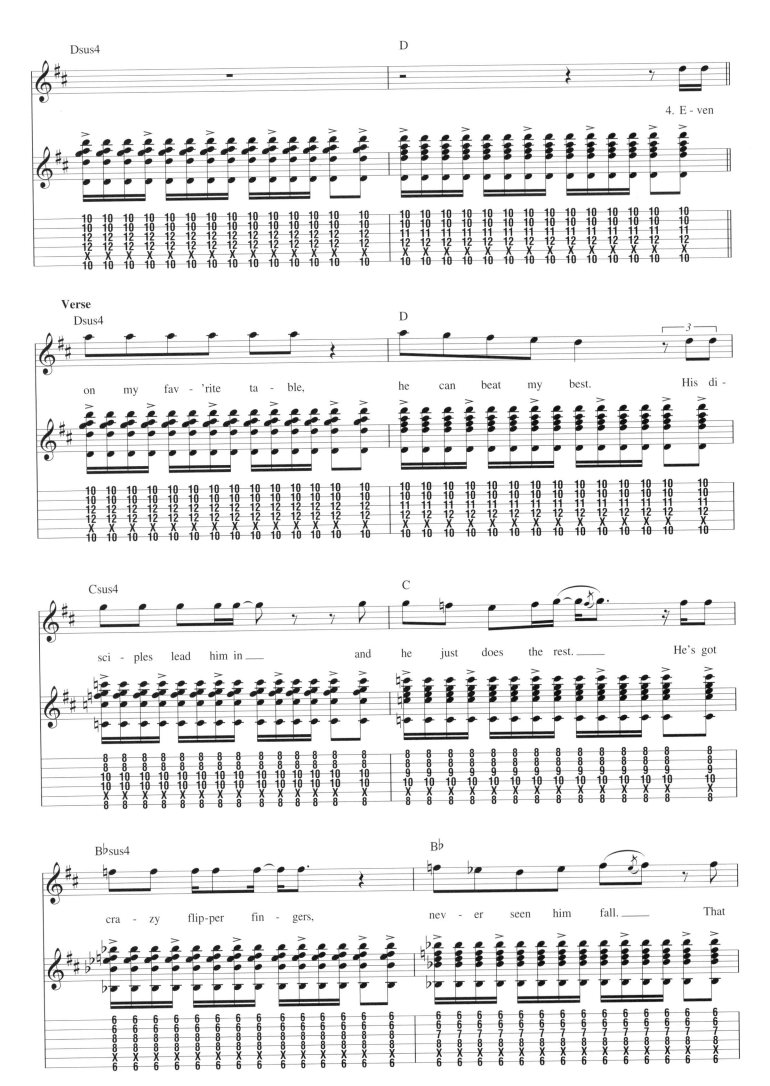

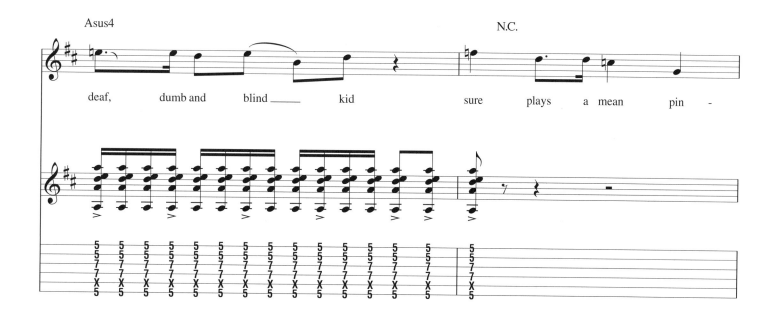

deaf,   dumb and   blind _____ kid   sure   plays   a   mean   pin -

Repeat and fade

Outro

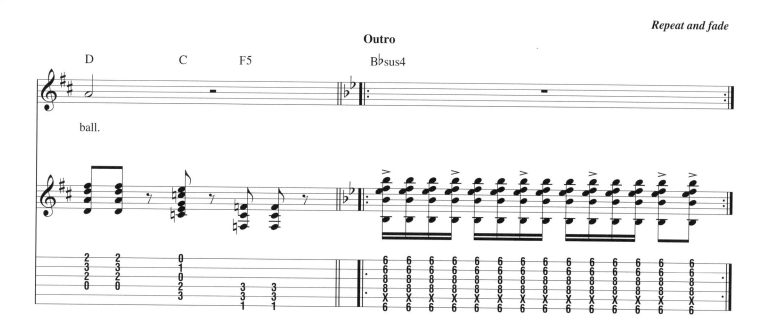

ball.

Additional Lyrics

2. He stands like a statue, becomes part of the machine.
   Feelin' all the bumpers, always playing clean.
   Plays by intuition, the digit counters fall.
   That deaf, dumb and blind kid sure plays a mean pinball.

3. Ain't got no distractions, can't hear no buzzers and bells.
   Don't see no lights a flashin', plays by sense of smell.
   Always gets a replay, never seen him fall.
   That deaf, dumb and blind kid sure plays a mean pinball.

Chorus   I thought I was the Bally table king
              But I just handed my pinball crown to him.

Smooth

Words by Rob Thomas
Music by Rob Thomas and Itaal Shur

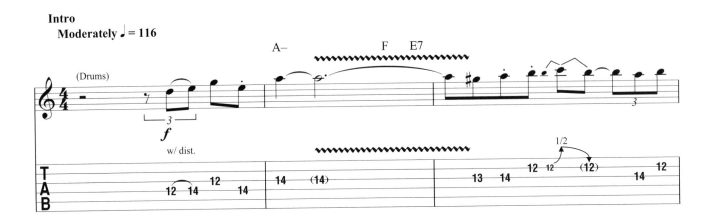

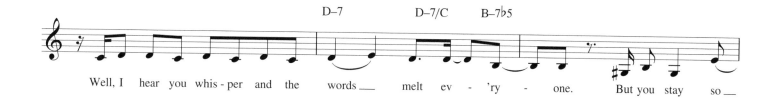

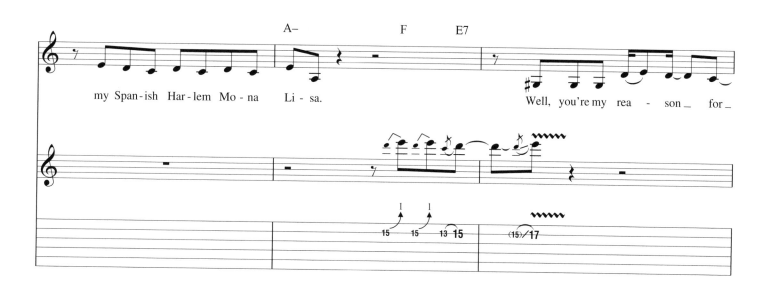

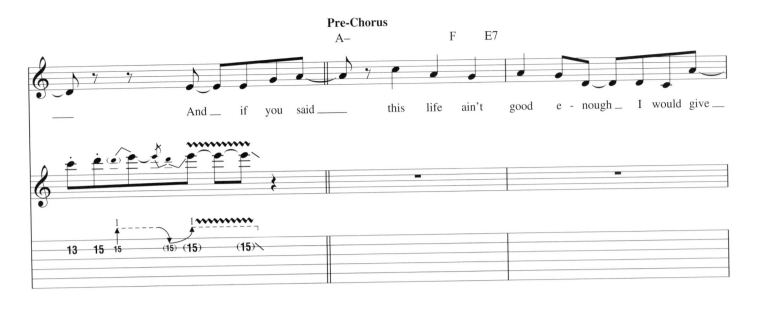

Pre-Chorus

And — if you said — this life ain't good e - nough — I would give —

_my world to lift you up. — I could change — my life to

bet - ter suit — your — mood, — yeah, be - cause you're so —

— smooth. — And it's just like the o - cean

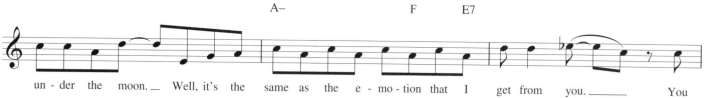

un-der the moon._ Well, it's the same as the e - mo - tion that I get from you._____ You

got the kind of lov - in' that can be so smooth, _ yeah. Gim - me your heart, _ make it real _

Interlude

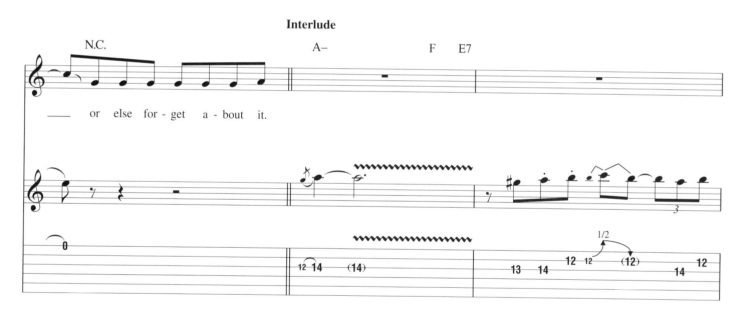

__ or else for - get a - bout it.

Verse

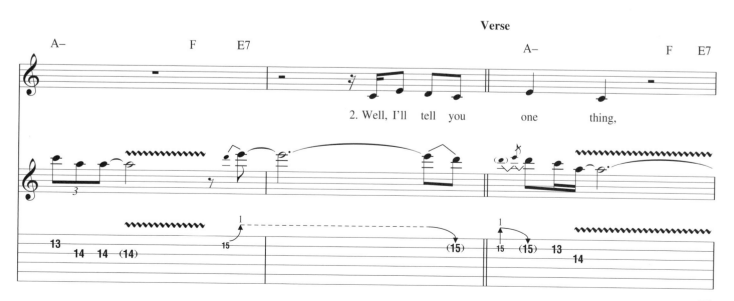

2. Well, I'll tell you one thing,

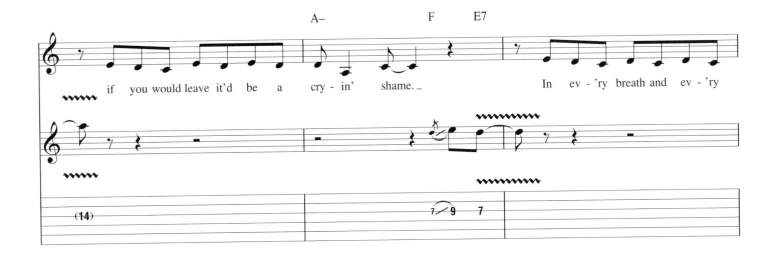

A–   F   E7

if you would leave it'd be a cry - in' shame. ___ In ev - 'ry breath and ev - 'ry

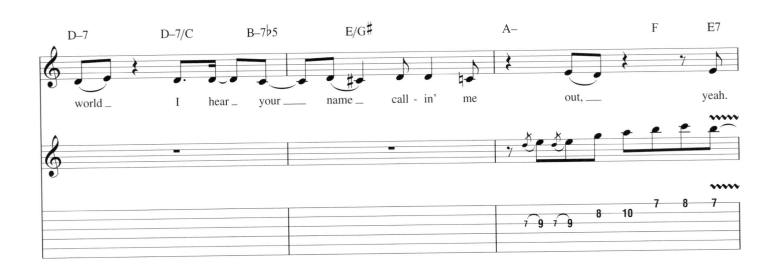

D–7   D–7/C   B–7♭5   E/G♯   A–   F   E7

world ___ I hear ___ your ___ name ___ call - in' me out, ___ yeah.

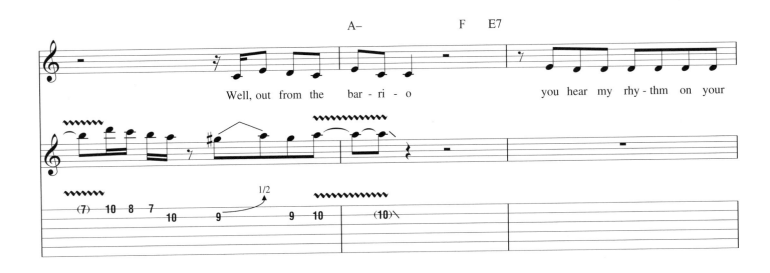

A–   F E7

Well, out from the bar - ri - o   you hear my rhy - thm on your

Gtr. tacet
A–   F E7   D–7   D–7/C   B–7♭5

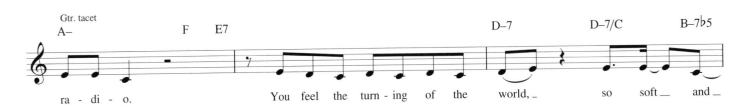

ra - di - o.   You feel the turn - ing of the world, ___ so soft ___ and ___

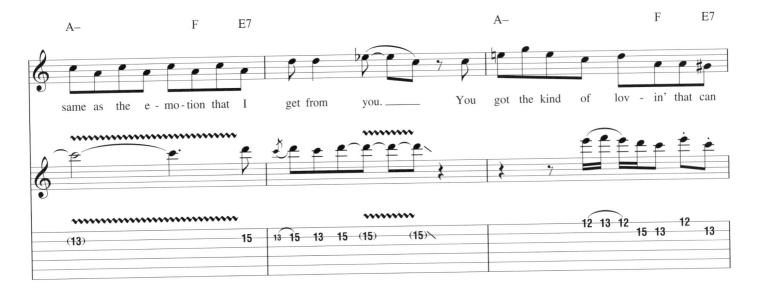

same as the e-mo-tion that I get from you.___ You got the kind of lov-in' that can

be so smooth, yeah. Gim-mie your heart,_ make it real,___ or else for-get a-bout it.

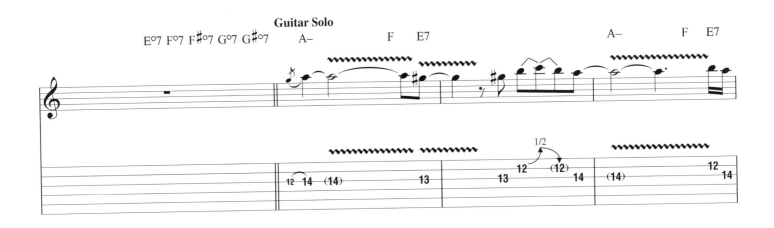

Guitar Solo

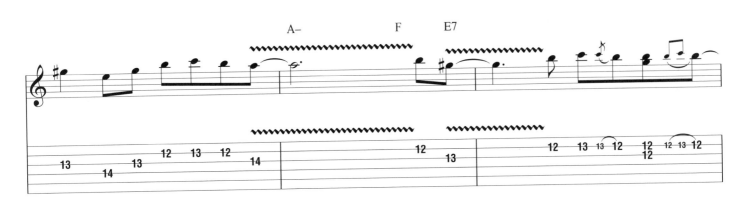

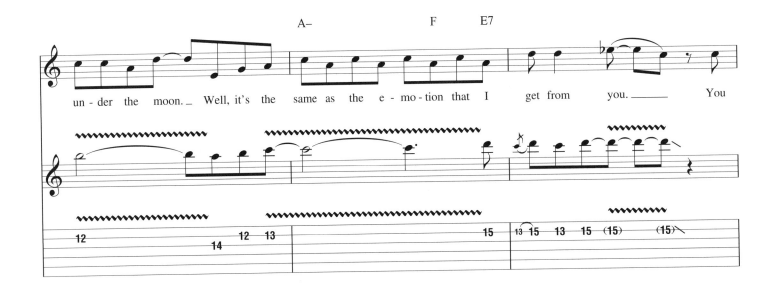

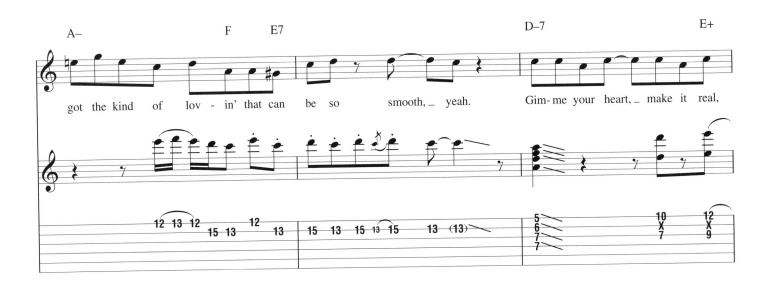

Outro-Guitar Solo

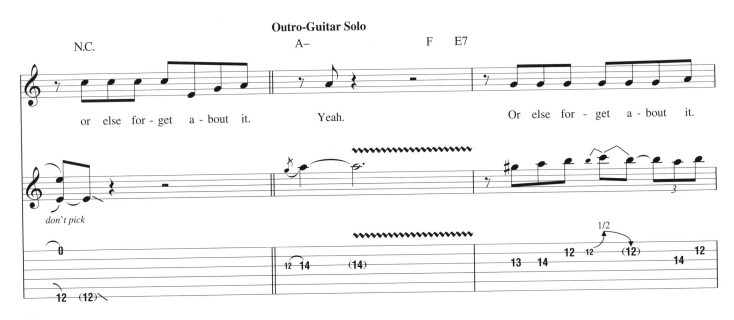

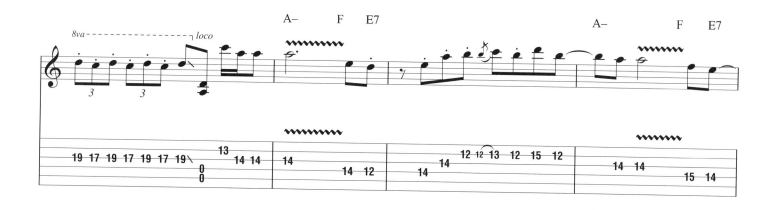

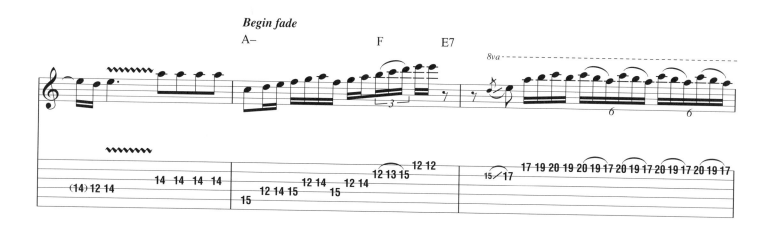

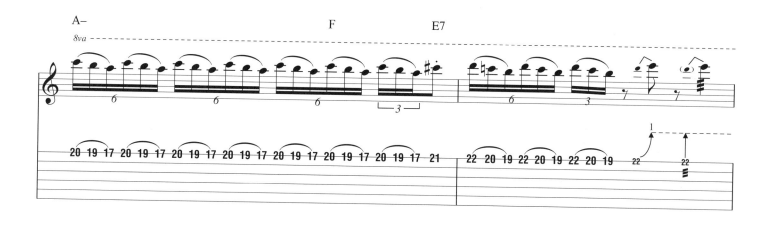

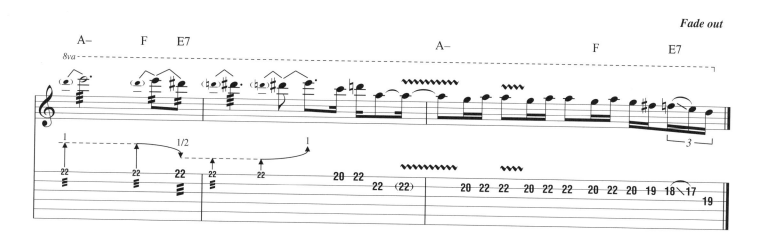

Up Around the Bend

Words and Music by John Fogerty

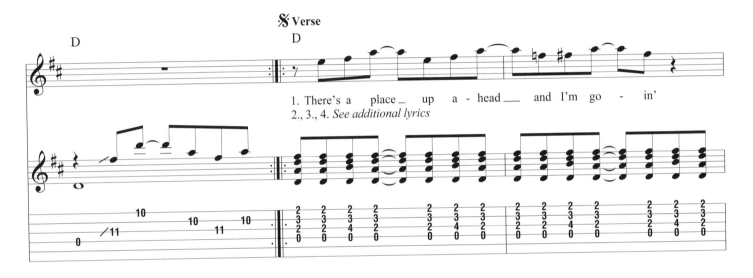

1. There's a place_ up a - head_ and I'm go - in'
2., 3., 4. *See additional lyrics*

just as fast_ as my feet_ can fly._ Come a - way,_ come a - way_

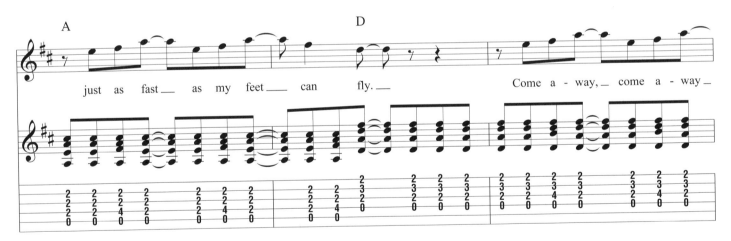

___ if you're go - in', leave the sink - in' ship_ be - hind._

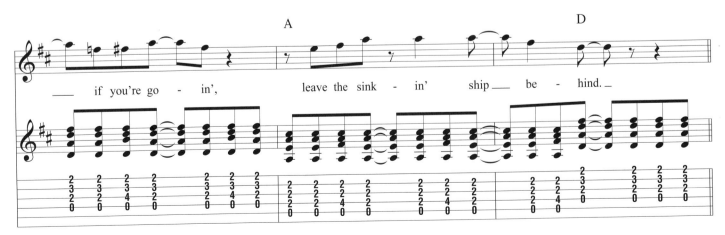

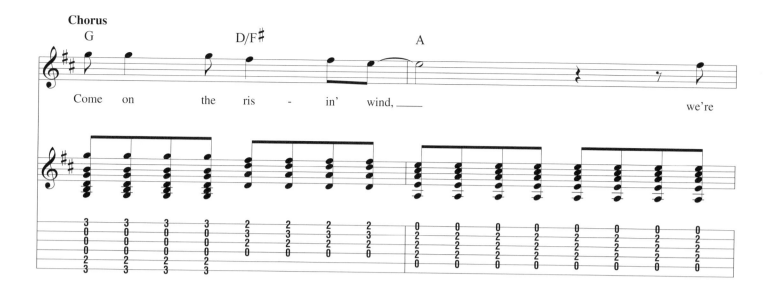

Come on the ris - in' wind, _____ we're

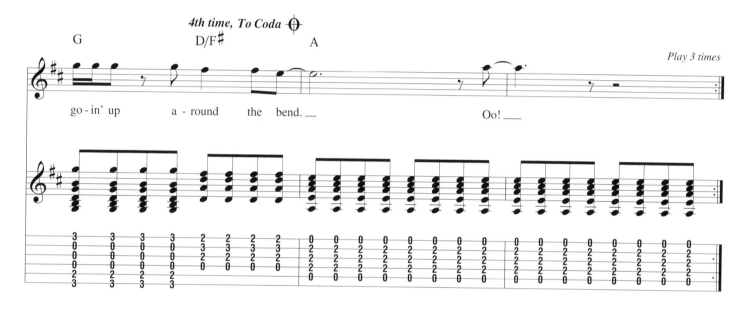

4th time, To Coda

Play 3 times

go - in' up a - round the bend. __ Oo! __

Interlude

Guitar Solo

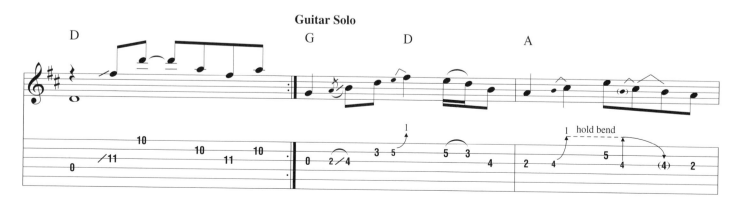

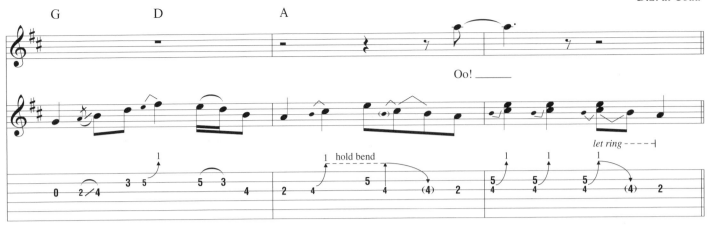

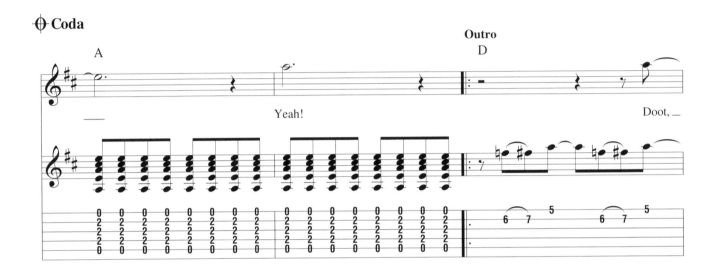

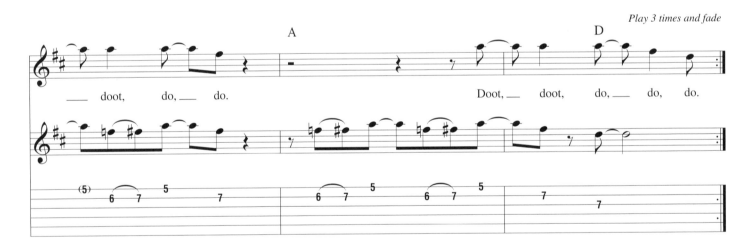

Additional Lyrics

2. Bring a song and a smile for the banjo.
   Better get while the gettin's good.
   Hitch a ride to the end of the highway
   Where the neons turn to wood.

3. You can ponder perpetual motion,
   Fix your mind on a crystal day.
   Always time for a good conversation,
   There's an ear for what you say.

4. Catch a ride to the end of the highway
   And we'll meet by the big red tree.
   There's a place up ahead and I'm goin';
   Come along, come along with me.

Sunshine of Your Love

Words and Music by Jack Bruce, Pete Brown and Eric Clapton

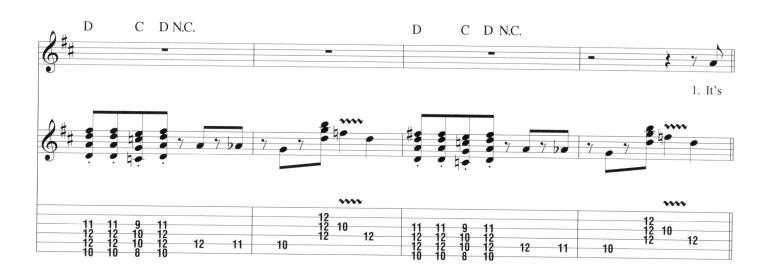

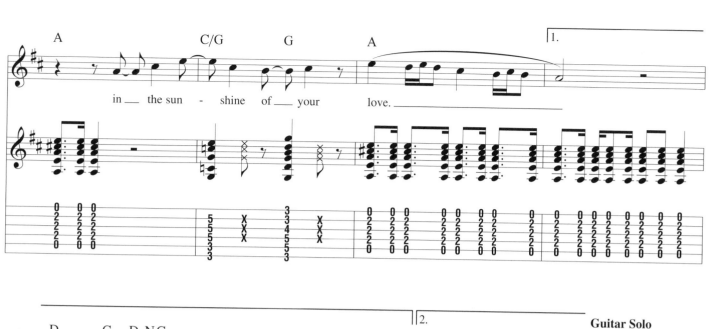

in ___ the sun - shine of ___ your love. ___

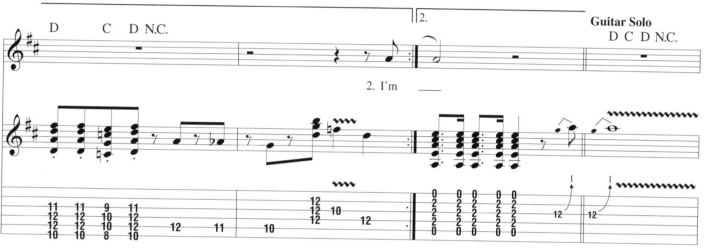

2. I'm ___

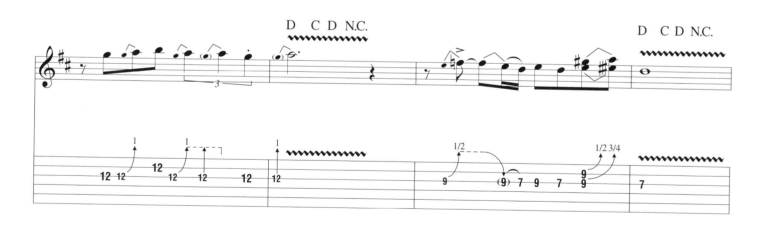

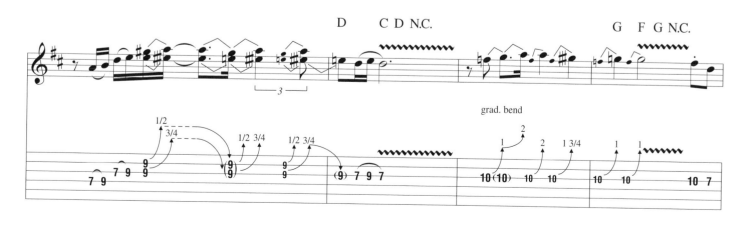

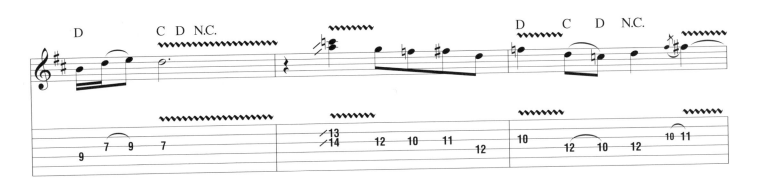

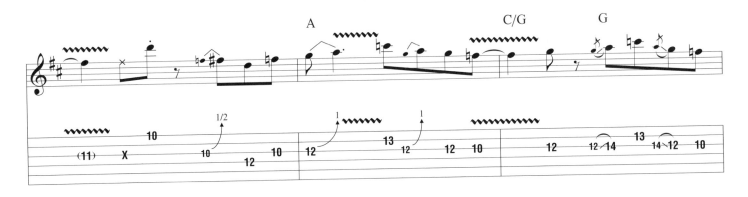

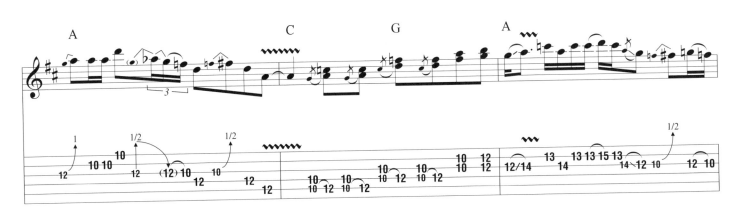

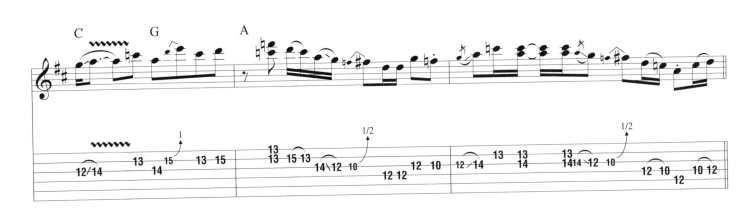

Additional Lyrics

2., 3. I'm with you, my love;
The light shining through on you.
Yes, I'm with you, my love.
It's the morning and just we two.
I'll stay with you, darling, now.
I'll stay with you till my seeds are dried up.

Wonderwall

Words and Music by Noel Gallagher

Capo II

Intro
Moderately ♩ = 87

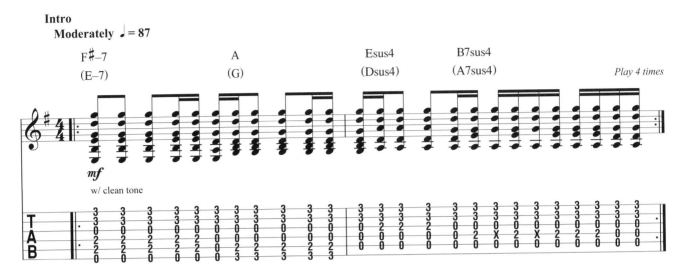

Verse

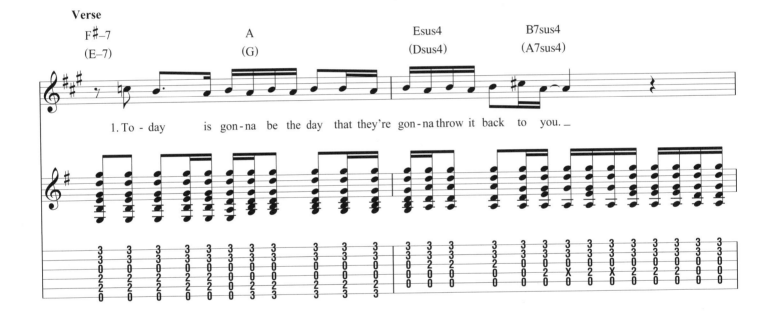

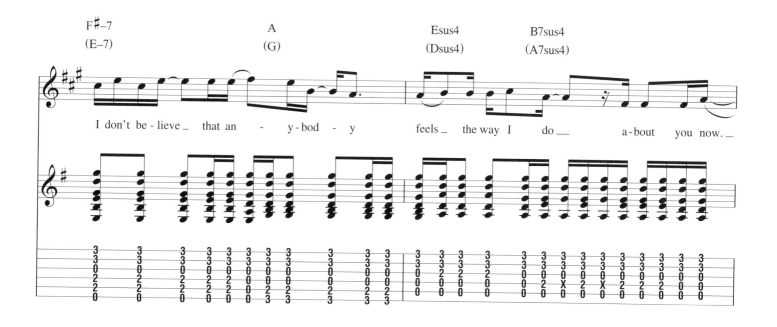

I don't be-lieve ___ that an ___ - ___ y-bod ___ - ___ y feels ___ the way I do ___ a-bout you now. ___

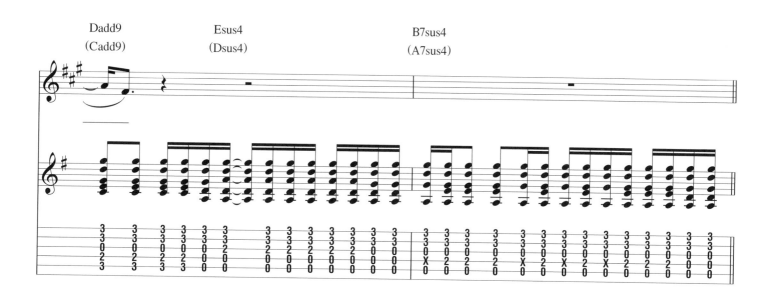

Verse

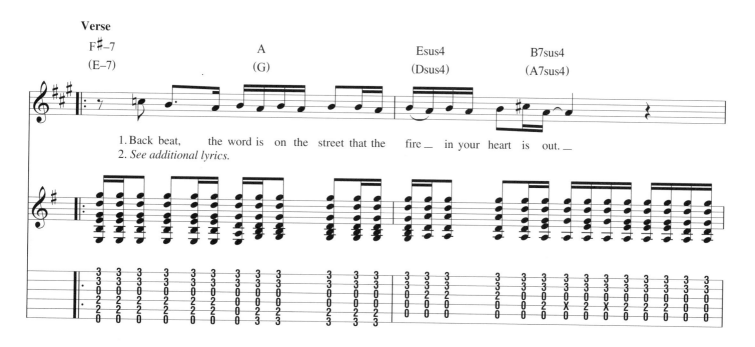

1. Back beat, the word is on the street that the fire ___ in your heart is out. ___
2. *See additional lyrics.*

I'm sure you've heard it all be-fore, but you nev-er real-ly had a doubt.

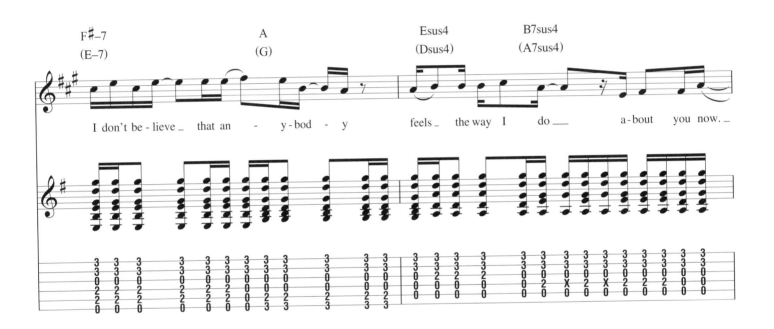

I don't be-lieve _ that an - y-bod - y feels _ the way I do __ a-bout you now. __

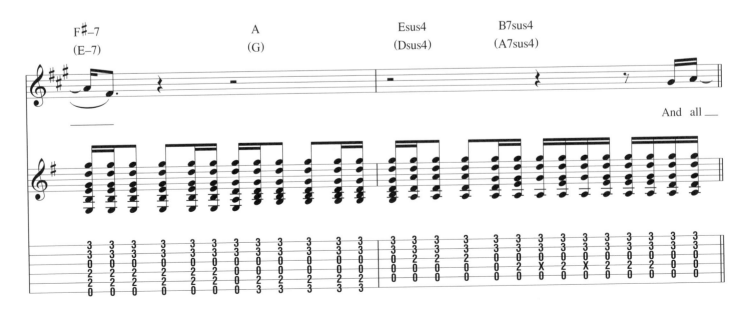

And all __

Pre-Chorus

— the roads _ we have _ to walk _ are wind - ing, and all _

let ring next 8 meas.

— the lights _ that lead _ us there _ are blind - ing.

There are man - y things _ that I ___ would like to say to you, _ by I don't know how _

Chorus

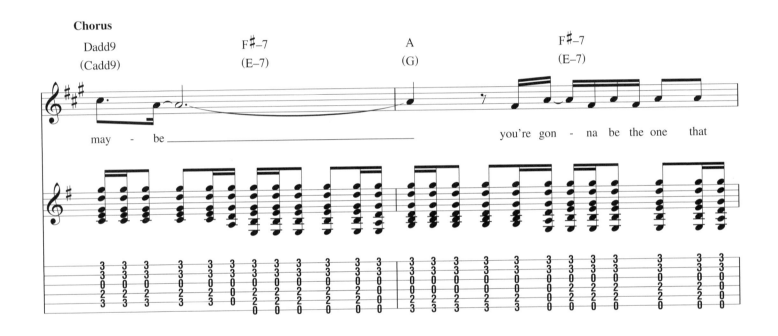

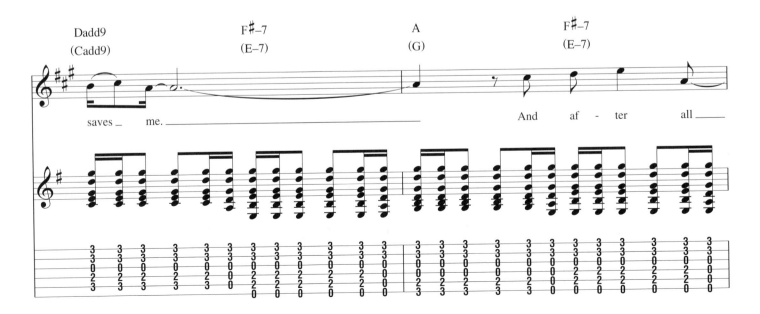

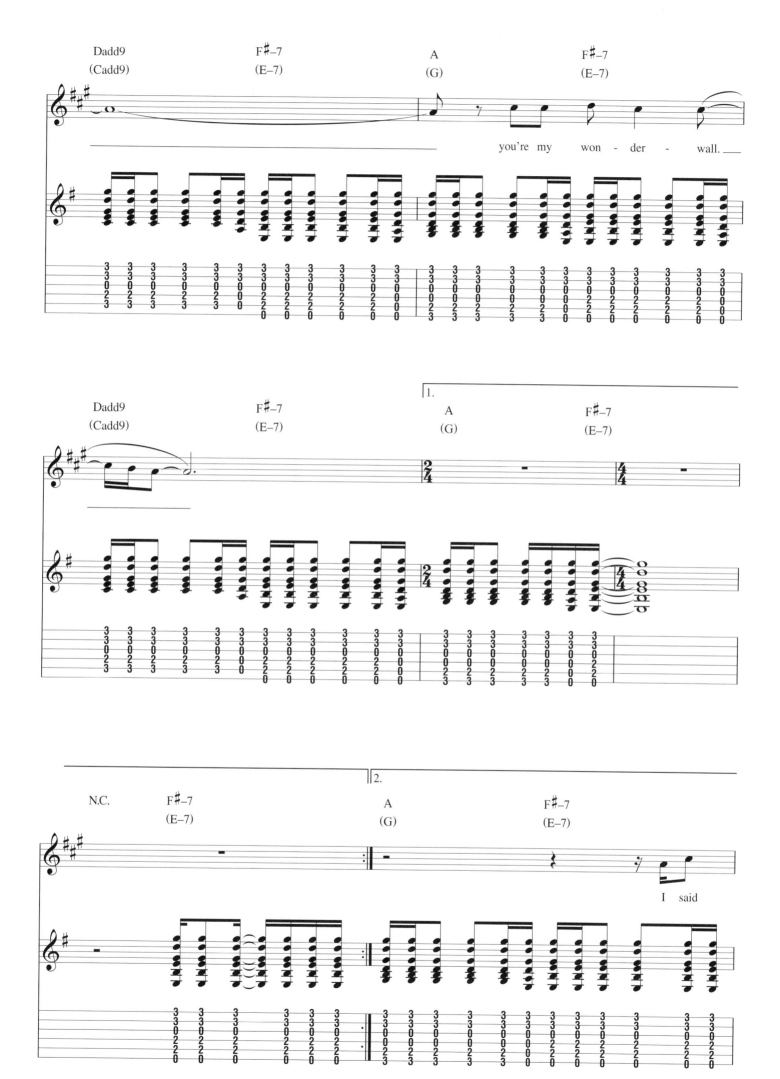

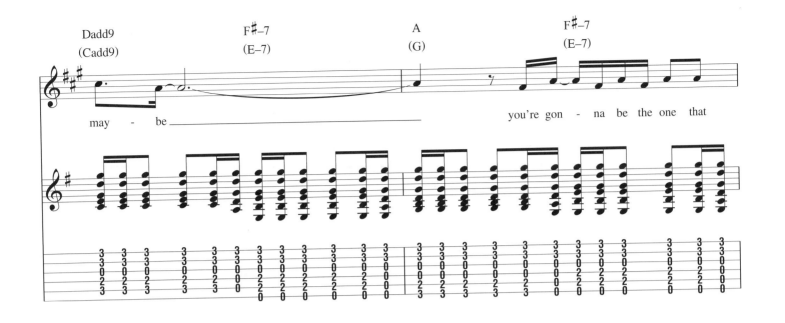

may - be _____ you're gon - na be the one that

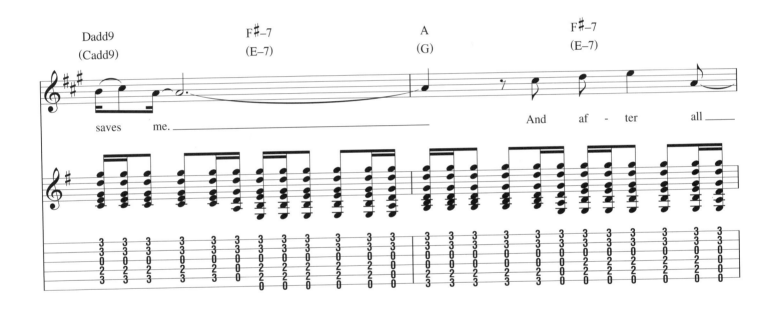

saves me. _____ And af - ter all _____

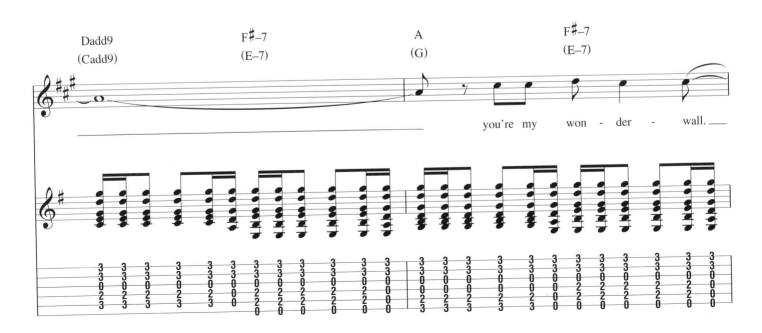

you're my won - der - wall. _____

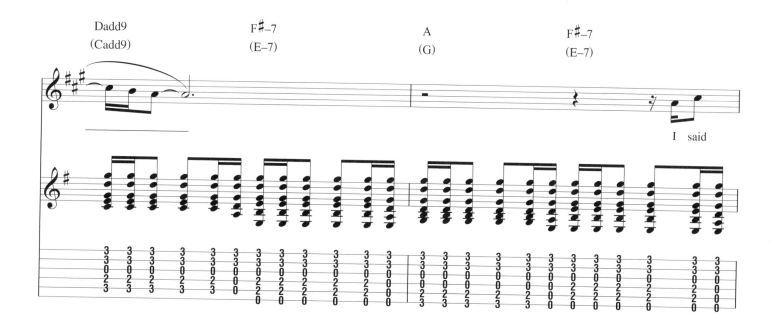

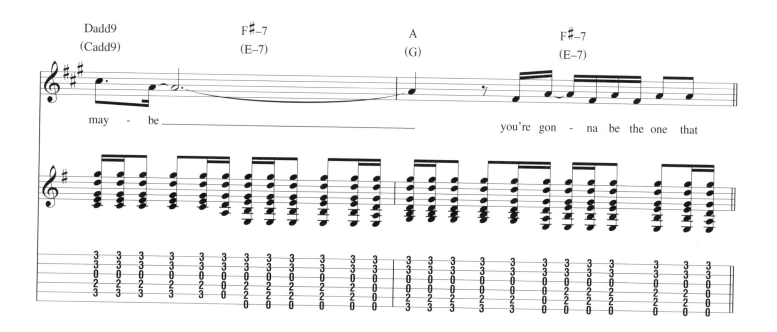

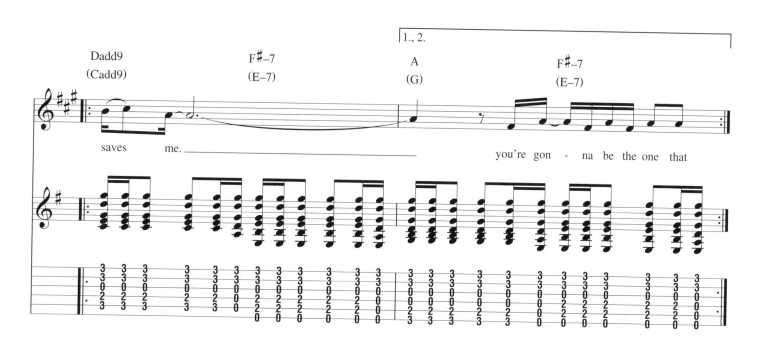

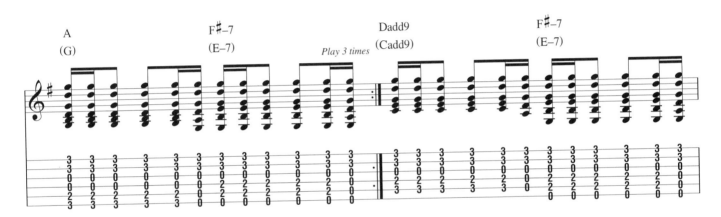

*Remove capo, placing gtr. in standard tuning.

Additional Lyrics

3. Today was gonna be the day, but they'll never throw it back to you.
By now you should have somehow realized what you're not to do.
I don't believe that anybody feels the way I do about you now.

Pre-Chorus And all the roads that lead you there were winding,
And all the lights that light the way are blinding.
There are many things that I would like to say to you,
But I don't know how.
I said...